Bird Watching at the End of the World

Bird Watching at the End of the World

Poems by Lisa Mangini

Cherry Grove

Published by Cherry Grove
P.O. Box 541106
Cincinnati, OH 45254-1106

ISBN: 9781625491015
LCCN: 2014948892

Poetry Editor: Kevin Walzer
Business Editor: Lori Jareo

Visit us on the web at www.cherry-grove.com

About the cover: "Plume," a collage by Kelly Green.

Author photo: Travis Lynn and Lori Lynn.

Acknowledgments

The author gratefully acknowledges the editors of the following publications in which the poems listed below first appeared, sometimes in an alternate version:

Knockout Magazine: "An Instant While Driving When I Imagine My Death"
American Journal of Nursing: "A Tour of the Lymphatic System"
Clockhouse Review: "Past the Solstice"
Fresh Ink: "One Hundred Days" and "I Must've Been Nikola Tesla in Another Life"
Louisiana Literature: "Homecoming" and "Why I Do Not Mind Driving Three Hundred and Eighty-Seven Miles"
Stone Highway Review: "Weathering"
Up the River: "A Bird in the Hand," "Bird Watching at the End of the World (i)," and "Upon Feeding a Pigeon in New York City"
Freshwater: "Letter to Descartes," "Einstein's Prophecy Loosely Penetrates My Nightmare," and "Matthew"
Soundings East: "The Statement"
Connecticut River Review: "Boundary"
Weave, "Every Time We Go to Ikea"
Mojave River Review: "The Logic of Childhood"

Selections of this book were first published in *Slouching Towards Entropy,* a chapbook published by Finishing Line Press, and *Perfect Objects in Motion,* a chapbook published by Red Bird Chapbooks.

Many thanks to Tim Parrish, Jeff Mock, Leah Nielsen, Edwina Trentham, Vivian Shipley, Robin Troy, and J.D. Scrimgeour for their guidance in the development of these works; to Kevin Walzer and Lori Jareo of Cherry Grove for this opportunity; to Kelly Green for the generous use of her art; with love to my parents Diane and Todd Mangini; and deepest thanks to Anand Swaminathan for his love, patience, and support.

Table of Contents

III. Bird Watching at the End of the World

I. Helium Balloon

An Instant While Driving When I Imagine My Death

In potent sunlight, in the cramped commuter lane,
six or eight years from now: I'm wearing wool
slacks, and dress shoes without scuffs. My car will
boast the latest safety features, but a profane
monthly payment. I adjust my sunglasses,
pop a cough drop, check my mirrors (where all I've
put behind me is closer than it appears) and pass
white-collared compatriots who've grown unkind:
all rock-hard trapezius, drained of laughter.
I'm singing—loudly, my entire lungs engaged
in my magnum opus, belted out to bootlegged
favorites, trying to stay young—then a deep gasp: disaster
forged by a menthol lozenge stuck mid-throat;
lane-coasting, faint, their blaring horns the final note.

A Tour of the Lymphatic System

The physician first washes
     his hands in the stainless
         steel sink. He moves to hold

his fingers to the back
     of her jaw, his skin smelling
         of triclosan soap. He presses,

and says *subparotid*.
     He is careful to look
         her in the eyes. He slides

both thumbs forward
     under her chin, pushes up:
         submental. Sweeping her long

hair away from her shoulders,
     he then reaches behind
         each ear along a bony stretch

of her skull. She remembers
     the diagram she found:
         The Lymphatic System

of the Head and Neck, the generic
    body in profile, strands
        of muscle ribboned in red

and blue. She pictures the dozens
    of yellow nodes dotting
        the body. They looked like mustard seeds,

or new buds clenched tight
    against a late spring. He cups
        her neck with one hand, feeling

for the *occipital* cluster. From there,
    he slides his hand down the path
        her lover's mouth took the night before:

hair line to collar bone.
    Her doctor takes his time here,
        as well, digging firmly into her tissue:

supraclavicular, inferior cervical,
    anterior deep cervical. She feels herself
        going lightheaded as he compresses

some kind of artery
    in this examination. *Almost done,*
        he tells her, as if in apology.

She can't stop thinking
    if he'll find some irregularity —
        is the criteria size, texture?

Each gland a firm bulb as it is;
    she recalls visits as a child,
        routinely told of their swelling

for strep throat, mononucleosis,
    an array of standard infections.
        He maps his hand up her shirt

to knead her armpit, the waxy film
    of her antiperspirant, the persistent sweat
        undeterred by it, her cells doing

what they do best: dividing again
    and again, perhaps a small glitch
        copied into each one.

Past the Solstice

He was most tempting in the summer,
when it's all matted grass and pollen, all
damp armpits; when light scrolls, delirious
and slow, across the wrinkled cliffs. I think
of him whenever I roll my shirt hem up
to mid-back, tucked in bra elastic, to ease
its cling to my skin. Past the solstice,
when acrid air squeals with impending rot—
soaked clothing in plastic bags, forgotten
crops—we'd thrash in mulch, or lay, limp
as infants, in brackish skin, mute, cedar
splinters in our hair. Grit-dusted, I'd pick
flecks of bark from bare arms; it's dangerous
to even keep the vaguest souvenirs.

This is Your Body Speaking (i)

You still make the same nervous joke
to the phlebotomist every time:
that you can't understand how
you can sit through three hours
of tattooing without the bat
of an eye, its needle vibrating
like a hummingbird. At first,
it didn't matter how many vials
of blood they took from the soft
hollow of your elbow — you would cry
long before the needle even touched

your skin. But now it's not so bad,
right? You learn to make anagrams
of the words printed on the box—
White latex-free gloves holds
so many possibilities: *reflex, wilt,
ghost* — come on, Mabel, you know
you found more than that last time
when they didn't draw half as much
from you. It's become a contest
with yourself, to see if you can beat
your own best average each time,
to hold back enough to not need
the Kleenex until you're jingling
the keys outside your car door.

When you leave today, you feel optimistic,
lighter almost, knowing as a fact
a few ounces of you, your blood,
has been siphoned out and away,
not quite sure where it will end up.
But you also know that, come tomorrow,
your skin will have grown a huge hibiscus
in that spot that will bloom for a full week,
that in the elbow's hinge it will feel
as if you're resting the strap of a heavy bag
across it, the same as it does
when you come home from the store
and have so much to juggle, to carry inside.

This is Your Body Speaking (ii)

It is impossible, you think, to identify
anything in this nearly all-black
celluloid of your guts. You think back
to tenth-grade biology, but can recall
only the stench of formaldehyde,
the serene look upon the piglet's face.
You think you recognize the white tines
of ribcage, the twin kidneys, the long
crinkled streamer of small intestine.
But on a large slab of gray, you see
the white mass — which you do not
recognize from any diagram —
round and obvious as the moon,
and somehow, whatever it is,
know it can shift the tide inside of you,
send everything swaying in its pull.

The Logic of Childhood

The worst birthday present I was ever given was a duffel bag full of lacy underwear. The best — that same year, age nine — was a label maker. The logic of childhood supports this. The favorite word of everyone under twelve is *mine.* The whole house covered in my name: jelly jar drinking glasses, the left and right canvas heels of my Keds, a doll-sized pink-plastic swimming pool. I already knew no sticker could adhere to the netted latticework of undergarments, knew I could not make known what was mine. A Barbie doll's head is made of Polyvinyl Chloride; her body is made out of something too hard to pronounce. She is more complex than any of us would've guessed, really. My parents took away all my Barbies once they caught me shearing off their hair, systematically, once scalp at a time. I would scatter the trimmings on the carpet, the white-blonde threads crisscrossed and shining like frost. They gave me string and beads, cardboard slats, glitter lined up in canisters like a spice rack. I spent six months hunched over the kitchen table, my after-school altar, making portraits of women: heart-shaped eyes or walrus tusks, a half-snake with sequined teeth, a tornado with a slanted bow. When my mother asked why I wanted a mirror, I told her even after all that practice, I still couldn't get my expression right.

Self-Portrait in a Public Restroom Mirror

It takes a moment to look up from my hands
covered in the froth of cheap soap, to see
my own face above the sink and under
the sign that insists employees do exactly

what I'm doing right now. I am uncertain
if the darkness beneath my eyes is evidence
of the four hours I slept this weekend, or
from the mascara I neglected to wash

away immediately before that brief
sleep. I configure my face into a smile,
and try to determine if I have good
cheekbones, if I have the slight beginnings

of crow's-feet or not. I have to admit,
my unwashed hair looks better today than most
days, and I am glad for it. I was never
quite aware how elegant good posture

could make someone appear until I jammed
my shoulders back in place, straightened my neck
with a few quick popping sounds. I recall
how much I love my one dimple, how much

I never wanted a cleft chin. Of all
the qualities I see, I wonder if—
when I'm not studying my face in smudged
glass, in a rest stop bathroom miles from home —

what I look like when I wince, or cringe
at laughing strangers, their inconvenient
joy that's not my own; how my eyebrows shift
that moment before a sneeze; or the expression

that may or may not ripple across this
face—I can only speculate, of course—
when he tells me he's made a terrible
mistake, that he needs me to stay,

and I don't even blink, not once.

This is Your Body Speaking (iii)

It is never the moon that emerges
from the cloudy water of the sink,
just stained plates that you long
to crack on the counter's edge.
Crickets no longer remind you
of tiny violinists congregating
at your front step. Abdomen,
thorax, exoskeleton, nothing.
Rubbing your eyes, you realize
people wish only on broken things:
lost lashes clinging to cheeks,
busted stars, the dry bone culled
from a poultry carcass. But Mabel,
you wonder what a wish even is,
the limitations of how one is defined
in stories as a kid, the consequences of one
slip in syntax coming to fruition
in a bad way. You wonder if you could
lean over your own flesh, wish upon
the asymmetrical organs, the suspect
blood, or if you have to see the damage
with your own eye for it to work its magic.

No One Ever Told Me

that an MRI sounds a bit like
avant-garde dance music, or one of those
key chains I had as a kid,

where I'd press a button
and it would shriek out some
distorted beeps and static to mimic

a machine gun, or a bomb falling
from far away. No one told me
that I should use those sounds,

count them to distract myself
from how long I'll have to hold
my breath. No one told me that nothing else

is as satisfying as the radiologist's
voice over the speaker system saying
OK, you can breathe now.

I felt like pork, driven into a dark tube,
the grinder, ready to be made into sausage.
I did not expect the radiologist

to be so kind when I writhed
on the first try. She patted me
with her cool hand and said *I'll give you*

a few minutes alone. How strange:
she, of all people, would be someone
I would want to call after with *Please don't*

leave me here alone. But after
I learned to keep my eyes shut,
as five years earlier, when he held

my shoulders down from above me, it became
somehow easier: I remind myself that I asked
to be here, planned it, calmly undressed

and left my clothes heaped
in another room. No one ever told
me that it would be an MRI — the strange

linens and the breathlessness — that would spin
me back to the memory of a blind date,
his empty house in the noiseless woods.

Will I exit this exam the same as I did that night:
gather my things casually, so stunned
that I smile politely and wave before saying goodbye,

overwhelmed by relief that it's over? But here,
in this office, it is not over yet:
when the long platform I'm sprawled on

surprises me with its quick jolt, like a stutter
forward and back, I clutch the sheet
beneath me, and focus on the noise:

discotheque, video game, fax machine,
the sound of an old ink jet printer
grinding the cartridge across

the page. No one ever told me
I would feel outside myself, as if I were standing
with my nose just above the paper, watching

the bands of color overlap one
thin strip at a time to form the whole
picture, waiting for it to finish.

My Subconscious Reminds Me Not to be Too Optimistic

Consider the time you were age six, on errands
with your mother: the lollipop from the bank
melting into one round sliver on your tongue,
the cardboard stick fraying from your spit.
Your mother urges you to hurry with her

into the supermarket, walk like a big girl,
but you are dawdling or half-skipping,
looking for pennies or acorns or a lost button —
some treasure in the parking lot, something
to keep in the flowered patch pockets of your dress.

When you are under the awning of the store's entrance,
you look up to see your mother inside with a cart.
The longer it takes you to get inside and catch up,
the more removed she will be, just selecting canned goods
from shelves above your head as if you did not exist.

You dash to the glass doors, but they do not open.
You press your hands to them, scratch and pry
at the center seam where the two panels meet,
even try pressing your lips to the surface, a gesture
of apology, as if you've wounded their pride

and want to make it better. You cry, *please, please,*
your little fists knocking. An older boy points, says
the automatic doors only work if you have a soul.
That's how they know to open. Watch —
and as he approaches, the crease you've been picking

with your fingernails spreads apart with a groan.
You run away from his laughter, inside, past the ends
of all the aisles, searching, and bury your face
in the bottom hem of her burgundy sweater
when you find her, nonchalantly sorting coupons

next to a large display of cereal on sale.
You hook your finger around the metal bar
of the cart, a way of steadying yourself against doubt.
After all the shampoo and ground beef and boxes
of spaghetti are arranged in their paper bags, you hide

behind your mother while exiting, afraid
of the door's dismissal a second time, afraid to know
for sure that your body is a helium balloon
four days after the party: an empty casing that somehow
lost this invisible thing that held it upright.

You follow your mother closely to the car, and while
you wait for her to pack all the bags into the trunk,
you think you spot a small pine cone next to the tire,
but it is only a rock. You scoop it up from the ground
and tuck it in your pocket — this will have to do.

This is Your Body Speaking (iv)

I am trying to be fair to you, Mabel,
to see it from your perspective. I know
you've heard the statistics: a single human
has something like sixty trillion cells, each
regenerating after seven years, give or take.

Do you remember being young enough
to still be afraid of such tasks as clipping
your nails, getting a haircut? We're all born
with that instinct to think it will hurt, to suspect it
unnatural to lose a part of yourself on purpose.
You then learned that a tooth left under your pillow
would result in a prize the next morning.
Your friends would miss class for procedures
like tonsillectomies, a ruptured appendix.

You stood outside your mother's operation room
as the surgeons removed a bloated ovary,
fallopian tubes, uterus, the whole system
ripped out — and she emerged groggy and sore,
but fine. You heard reports of two full feet
of your cousin's faulty intestine removed,
an aunt's gallbladder, both of a co-worker's breasts,
a friend's uncle who kept only the better half
of his scarred liver. A former Vice President
could save his ailing heart with valves borrowed

from pigs. Of course you're confused at how
this soft vessel you're trapped in matters,
if it's such a threat after all when parts malfunction.

But just think of the year your father
was unemployed and parted out the '74
lime green Plymouth Demon for extra cash,
how you'd come from school each day, cataloging
which pieces had disappeared from the frame propped on
cinder blocks: headlights, grill, chrome trim,
both bucket seats, rear quarter panels, till one day —
you are not sure when — you approached your driveway
and decided, in your 13-year-old judgment,
that what was left could only be considered metal.

The Last Meal

I would start with a glass of Merlot,
despite that I have never enjoyed wine
solely on the principle that I am simply
not sophisticated enough. Nonetheless, please,

fetch me a corkscrew; it is never too late
to become a little graceful, refined; to
improve oneself, no matter how little time
is left to improve. I would request French

Toast made of Challah with margarine,
imitation maple syrup, sprinkle cinnamon
before sawing each bite from the whole
like a piece of meat. Now that I think of it,

I may even order a nice cut of something
medium rare after my abstaining from beef
right around the same time I stopped abstaining
from sex. Since it's the end, I would dip

French fries into chocolate milkshakes, followed
by a dish of plain, quartered artichoke hearts,
inspecting each of the tender leaves inside
as if they might contain a secret truth.

As that final time approached, if I still
held the vacancy to contain it, I would consume
zipper pulls from my favorite dresses, leaves
from the white birch in my childhood front yard, grind

my teeth on seashells combed from vacation beaches.
I would place eyelashes from my true love
on my tongue like tabs of acid, swallow
fireflies, the down of baby swans. I would

place all of these things inside of me,
and be nourished by them, feel them
sustain me, the same way as always,
through the last of this quiet unfulfillment.

Chronology

I remember my grandmother backward—last
June: hospitalized, bruised wrists from intravenous,
gasping, white-gowned, my father still grasping
her hand, and that she's long past precarious.
Next, it's my fifth Christmas: a rare trip to Springfield,
my fingers jammed in her sagging couch layered
with egg crate foam, as I stutter-read Shel Silverstein,
praised through sips off her inhaler. If I continue,
I reach a place before myself: 1966, my father aged
twelve, plucking a guitar, perched next to her
in the car's front seat, as she carted him to a friend's
garage after my grandfather denied the ride:
the story he made sure I heard, giving leverage
to the living, a way we can revise her end.

II. All the Electric Novelty

Upon Meeting a Physicist for Dinner

"What was the necessary condition for making the thing
conceived this time into you, just you and not someone else?"
- Erwin Schrödinger

I know if I look up at Andrew's face, my dish
of pasta will not be replaced by some other entrée
and then shift back when I return my fork
and focus to my plate. Still, I can't help thinking:

is our first date going all wrong in some parallel plane
where I am more brazen, one where I let him see me
grinning instead of pulling handfuls of my scarf
across my lips to hide my nervous laughter?

Soon he will leave this table and this town, to study
the way sound behaves in an almost-empty space,
and how a sound, despite its frequency, only takes
a bit of matter to change its silent movement

and turn into song. If I were not so concerned
over his next destination—a choice between Texas
and Pennsylvania—would he choose the place
closest to me? I want Schrödinger's cat to survive

the radiation in the glass vial, waiting for it
beneath the tiny suspended hammer — it will
as long as none of us open the crate to see
for ourselves. It's easier to say I'm fascinated

by this science which tells us that the unexamined particle
is not a particle, but a wave — that the moment
he and I are content to look away from each other's
blushing faces, under a veil of photons from streetlights

above our heads, we already suspect the possibility
will materialize before us. When we turn
to face each other again, we will know as fact
the exact location of our hands and mouths.

Appetite

She did not think it would be this easy
to fall, to feel a swell of delight in a place
called "The Chowder Pot." He traces
circles on her creased skin, her palms upturned
and open as two half-shell mussels. He teases
her about the décor: suspended lobster traps,
fishing nets, hurricane lamps with faint sputters
of light under all that pooling wax. The apples
of her cheeks turn the color of her salmon — she wants
to know if she is flush from wine, the shame
of having him bring her twenty miles for a cutlet
of pink fish only to please her, the arousal
of his fingernail orbiting slow over the clustered
veins of her arched wrist, eavesdropping on her pulse.

One Hundred Days

is enough time for fourteen dinners out
on Friday nights, linking his arm and sauntering
down Washington Street under a blue-white moon,
the fickle early spring which calls for both
open windows and heavy blankets as we sleep,
pressed beside each other, his arm draped
over the fleshy transition of my waist and hip. It is

enough time for a day trip to an art museum
in the Berkshires, my chin resting
on his shoulder, whispering of colors
and shadows into his ear, my fingers
tracing the velvet rope barricade placed
between us and masterpiece, an elegant
reminder not to get too close. One hundred

days is long enough for me to wear three
different sweaters of his on breezy nights,
or the black blazer he would rest atop
my shoulders, tell me the combination
of it paired with my flowered sundress and
oversized sunglasses made me appear
classic, timeless, straight from the silver screen
of the 1950s. One hundred days

is enough time for me to calculate
mentally or on my hands, picturing
the grids comprising the remaining months
of April and May, or the little squares
peeled from the calendar like the petals
of a daisy when a small girl pulls it
to pieces to determine if she is loved.

Crossing the Hudson

I remember my first time: westbound, white-knuckled,
my radio turned up high as if I could use pure sound,
its vibrations, to push the fear from my car and out

my open window, float between the metal trusses
crossed like argyle, and land in the three miles-wide
of water below, like a penny tossed in a fountain

for good luck. It is for this reason I can count
on one hand how many times I've paid
the five-dollar fee to leave New Jersey and drive

the Tappan Zee to take me home. I much prefer
the travels that send me further upstate, the quaint
Newburgh-Beacon: modest, not as dizzying —

after some practice, I could start to loosen up
my clenched hands, to love the word "cantilevers."
Even the Dutch suffix "-kill" has grown charming

to me. But mostly it's the time I scraped my nails
against the inside of my wallet, dug along the bottom
seam of my cotton handbag, raked my palm beneath

the driver's seat only to amass a gum wrapper
and eighty cents worth of the dollar toll back east.
I pulled up to the booth embarrassed, braced

for consequences as the attendant smiled wide,
her blonde hair bouncing as she waived and nodded:
Go ahead, Sugar, that car in front of you paid your toll.

Homecoming

Tailgating is a serious event in this town. Despite
the invite to grill burgers and drink beer, pretend
we know anything about football, we sleep late,
long past ten, then noon, rolling over towards
each other upon waking and sensing the six-inch
space between our bodies from drifting apart

between dreams. It is like us, really:
spending weeks apart, then drawing back together
the first instant we are able. When we wake,
it's almost comical: we take turns burying our noses
at the crown of each other's head, the nape of the neck,
or even close to an armpit, taking in the scent
as if we could store it inside ourselves, save it
for later. I watch Andrew in front of the bathroom mirror,
working a damp hand through his bedhead hair. I tug
at the shoulder of his bathrobe, rub his back, my affectionate
way to rush him to get dressed without saying so.

He drives us past the downtown, everything deserted:
the golf course, the two waffle shops, the YMCA
on University Drive — I feel something like accomplishment
when it occurs to me I know these places, these street names,
even as a recurrent guest — and then past the parking lot
of the stadium, crowded with cars, windshields bouncing light
back at us like hundreds of sequins. We keep going,

drive through three counties — it's as if we have grown
so used to being behind the wheel, on our way
to or from somewhere, that it seems fitting to travel
somewhere else together: through the valley sprinkled
with cows, further past woods, out near the Amish,
their worn clotheslines and hay rakes in the yard.
It's October in its prime, no matter where we go —
crisp air, wood smoke, how they braid together before us,
drift west and north and everywhere, a suggestion
that there is no necessity to return anywhere.

Every Time We Go to Ikea

it's raining. It starts as a light spray
across the windshield, so slight the wipers squeal
against the glass. But there's no fighting

against the allure of clean lines, the illusion
of better organization, despite that no
number of cubed shelves can tidy up a life.

And every time, there is a young woman
assessing the sturdiness of a crib, sometimes alone,
sometimes with a man or her mother beside her,

and I do my best not to meet your eyes. Every time
we weave through the model kitchens, I make a bee line
to the sink — farm apron, stainless steel, undermount —

and press my palms against its cool basin; if it's not
crowded, you'll lean your hips along my back, rest
your chin on my shoulder, trying to see what it is

I'm seeing. We'll look for a chest of drawers
for your apartment, debating *Malm* versus *Hopen*,
birch finish or espresso, and I'll scribble

their dimensions in inches with a tiny golf pencil.
We'll emerge with a cardboard box on a dolly
to a downpour, and against your wishes, I'll insist

on moving the car to the loading area myself. Every time,
I will lose a sandal while running in the slick lot
and have to turn back to retrieve it. We'll maneuver

the box in some impossible diagonal in the back seat
of the sedan, wipe the rain from our faces, prepare
ourselves to go home and build something.

Celestial

Curled in plastic furniture and the aftermath
of one gratuitous glass of wine, I wonder
if Andrew's sleeping yet: bent, on his left side,
leaning into something soft, face adjacent

to pillow, hands holding chin, the blanket
I knit for him tucked between his knees.
It is not unusual for him, at half past
eleven, to still be hunched over a desk

in the lab, doing whatever it is
that he does. I cannot envision much
beyond his posture, the desk itself,
a mechanical pencil resting in his hand.

I want to find a way to pull him from his focus,
allow him to relax. Perhaps he is home, perhaps
he woke for water, not bothering the light switch,
staggering down the hall. Could he have seen the meteor,

spun past his kitchen window, the one
compelling me to stop, to speculate
the sequence of his sleep, the routine of his day,
all the things I can't influence from this distance.

Weathering

He wonders why she has run out of his home, barefoot and jacketless, to stand outside in the cold, watch the passing cars, then return a few minutes afterward, pissed and shivering: "I am more unhappy than you know. I could leave you, you know. I could." She sits on the couch, sticks her hands beneath her thighs to try warming them. So she is unhappy? The way she linked her pinky finger in his belt loop all last night at the party, saying: "I don't think it's fair to rub our love in everybody's face." But she says now "you don't take my pain seriously — there is something wrong in my body, and not one of those doctors is sure what it is."

He blinks, looks down, knows there is not one thing he can say to soothe her. She grabs his arm with her still-cold hand and he feels a chill ripple through him. It reminds him of last Christmas when he went home to see his parents. He shoveled two feet of wet snow and cleared off the old Toyota and helped his one-hundred-and-six-pound father navigate the icy stoop and drove him all the way to Trenton so he wouldn't miss his dialysis. He can see her struggling to find the right way to hold her head, the right angle to make eye contact with him, asking "Do you see what I mean now? Do you see how easy it is for me to not feel supported when you shut me out?" He remembers his father opened a letter from the hospital when they got home, seeing glimpses of words like *critical, malignant, oncologist, metastatic.* He watched his father cross through his Social Security number from beneath the letterhead with a magic marker, refold it into thirds, shimmy it back into the envelope, drop it into the recycling bin. He remembers trying to reach in after the letter, to reread it in his own hands instead of over his father's shoulder. His father grabbed him at the wrist, his serious eyes communicating he was not to touch it. His father squatted to pick up the plastic bin, let out a quick grunt, and thrust it at him: "Here. Take this to the curb. We don't need your mother worrying over things we can't change." He put on his boots. His father called after him, waiving a black knit cap, warning him not to get sick. He shuffled through slush to the end of the driveway, and pushed the plastic bin into the darkened snow. He could see the black line of the nine-digit number struck through with Sharpie. He bent down, cupped the snow in his hands over and over, until the paper disappeared beneath it.

She grabs his shoulder, sobbing: "Look at me! Why can't you understand all I want is some empathy? Don't you know how frightening something this ambiguous is?" He wants to tell her ambiguity is a luxury. He looks past her face as he offers his sleeve to wipe the dribbling from her eyes and nose, out the window into November sky at four in the afternoon — already so much like dusk — and knows how cold and short the days will be, knows the snow will be coming soon.

Ambiguity

The pine trees bordering his apartment tower above her, look threatening at night in her rearview mirror, their sagging boughs dark as if dipped in road tar. It starts snowing lightly — Mabel can only tell there are flakes at all by the small drops on her windshield. There'll be nothing to look forward to for a long time. Tomorrow she'll stay at home, in the quiet, perusing Kierkegaard for her own studies. He'll return to his lab and think of nothing but numbers and variables for days. She looks out the window at the city, and how even for Sunday it seems especially still, so many houses with darkened rooms, only semis to share this interstate. Up ahead, she sees a configuration of lights, unsure of what they are. She never noticed before, most likely because it was not dark enough, too crowded with cars to look away from the road. The lights get closer, still only vague shapes of something she can't make out. It must be festive strands wrapped around a row of trees, the way the light is shaped like a row of incandescent bulbs, or upside-down heads of garlic, segmented cloves like fingers on hands in prayer. They could almost be umbrellas. Mabel feels like this is all she does all day: try to figure out something from far away and test her accuracy the closer she approaches. From this distance, the lights remind her of a row of flower buds closed up tight, like so many rhododendrons, uncertain if they will open come spring.

Why I Do Not Mind Driving 387 Miles

I am close: I can see the silhouette of silos,
the loose-beamed fences lining the road
under this fresh dusting of decorative snow,
the pasture by the highway still dotted with cows
kneeling on their folded legs, even at dusk,
not yet herded into the barn. Twenty-two miles
to go, and Andrew is already watching for me
out his kitchen window, ready to put on his boots,
carry in my overnight bag for me. Sometimes
I wonder if he spends all six hours there, hand
on the windowsill, looking for my car to appear.

After thirteen days apart, he looks me over
at arm's length, assessing my gaze and the curve
of my neck as I remove my coat and stretch;
he watches my mannerisms to make sure
four hundred miles have not altered me. There are always
just a few minutes of quiet glances, tentative gestures
while we readjust to the presence of each other,
easing in to this return. I believe it is involuntary
for my mind to search my past for the last time
I may have felt something akin to this: thirteen,
after dark, under the eaves of a department store?
Sixteen, slamming the door of a rusted sedan?
Perhaps, but would he have recognized me then,
observing me at arm's length, without the way

I am now, having known him? He unclasps
the hook-and-eye of my silk dress, lifts it from me,
smoothes the hair he's tangled. The quiet shifts
like a moth flitting close to the streetlamp:
constant, sustaining, diffuse. In this dim light,
the only parts of me that exist are the parts of us
pressed together — *sentio ergo sum* — or rather,
I feel *Andrew*, therefore I am. To think, I've missed
these pieces of myself for days and not noticed, was unaware
there was so much of me left here that could not
be shuffled into shoulder bags and carried back.

Lemonade on the Fourth of July

Three pounds of lemons in a mesh yellow bag sit on the passenger's seat as she reverses out of his driveway: a dozen in all, one lemon for each hour spent driving for this visit: six out, six back. He could not fathom why she so desperately wanted these lemons, so many. He called her frivolous, but tossed them into the cart regardless. She wanted something—just one thing—that could be spontaneous, that didn't need to be scheduled in advance. While still daylight, she smelled their scent: faint citrus wafting through the car, sun-baked by windows. Flashes of fireworks burst and melt in the sky over the highway, like hundreds of white moths gathering in the shape of a cheerleader's pom-pom, shaken open and full. *Let's go, let's go, L-E-T-S-G-O.* How nice to enjoy their effervescence without the noise, the crowds. How simple and easy things are for her now. Last Independence Day was her first I-love-you to him — six months in: on a beach towel at the Jersey Shore, having met his parents the night before. It had to be safe now, yes? And yet, it hurried out like a whimper from Pandora's box, something pained about it, and she's never been sure why. The smell of soot filters through the vents; the air like someone struck a whole box of matches at once. It reminds her of the cigarettes she used to smoke, the strong drink perched in her hand during these occasions, an occasional party joint — everything she's given up to make him happy. Once home, she cuts each lemon down the center, strains her fingers, squeezes out juice. The seeds, firm and slippery, are not unlike Tic-Tacs in her mouth, as she glides them around her teeth — an impulse not understood, but still satisfying, in a way. Her cuticles burn, stinging and sticky. The grit of sugar feels like sand; she wonders if she'd ever adjust to his landlocked home. The thought of it makes her want to drop everything and drive to the ocean, this instant, only 20 minutes south. But she made such a fuss about this lemonade, and now she's committed to seeing it through. She stirs a wooden spoon through the pitcher, and laughs a little, recalling the saying, *when life gives you lemons,* despite that she purchased these very lemons on purpose. She wanted to transform something. Her phone rings, and she knows that he's calling to make sure she's home safely. The answering machine fills her kitchen with his voice: "Mabel, just wanted to check in and make sure you made it OK. Can't wait to see you again." Just hearing him makes her shoulders go slack, as she imagines him rubbing her back as he so often does. She tells herself to shake it off; it won't be long before he realizes he's too good for her. She strikes a match, breathes deep, and lights a candle. As she grabs ice for her glass, she notices the horizontal vodka bottle in the freezer —for "special occasions"— but thinks better of it, despite the holiday. He'd be disappointed. She gathers up the yellow rinds from the cutting board, tossing them one by one into the trash. In the morning, her whole house will smell like furniture polish, or dish soap; she will wake to a home that feels empty and clean.

Wisdom of the Body

"There is more wisdom in your body than in your deepest philosophy." — Friedrich Nietzsche

There was the time at the river, an hour before dusk,
when I squinted into the sky just to look
away from him, said I thought I saw a hawk.
I needed something to help keep my mouth shut:
who wouldn't be tempted to say something stupid

at the sight of water reflecting pink and orange,
birch boughs — so white almost neon — slender
and swaying at the river's edge? I was convinced
it could mean nothing, that it was unwise to trust
Andrew's hand taking mine and guiding me
over the mud and wet stones back to the car.

There was the evening walk after dinner,
the clearing salted with the blink and shimmer
of fireflies, how I said it reminded me of the light
reflected from a mirrored ball hung above a dance hall,
and so he put his arms around my waist and swayed me,

side to side. Here, too, I tensed: dusk and dogwood
blossoms, our tongues stained dark with tannins,
the taste of shiraz on our breath — it felt suspicious.
Spring and wine, and suddenly I'm sure? I weighted it,
considered the evidence, observed the path
of the green-lighted bugs in the field, silent, until
he pulled me closer, offered his jacket in the unexpected
chill of May, and we returned inside. But not him—

he never analyzed the water's color, or the tiny beams
of light shining from a flying bug. He never flinched
at helping me to his car for a doctor visit, my breath
of chicken stock and Dimetapp and stale drool.
Waking beside me, he never hesitated to wrap
an arm around me, rest a cheek against my back,

and fall back into sleep, as if instinct. Even now,
I ask about the day we met, how he reached
across the café table for my fidgeting hands,
and said *I just had to touch you. I can't explain it,
I just needed to.* I ask him what that even means,
how he recognized that impulse and followed it.

He tells me it must be like the time I finally knew,
after six months of not ever saying it: July, at the beach,
feet scalded by sand, crowded with huge shirtless men
and screaming kids; when I sipped my watery iced coffee,
wrapped myself around his greasy, sun-screened back,

and whispered to him without thinking, without even
needing to look in his eyes. Instead I followed his stare
at the waves tripping themselves, and beach-goers flinging
their towels behind them and wading into the cold Atlantic,
unable to repress their shrieks at the sensation of the water.

Horseshoe Curve

He wanted to bring Mabel to see it, to be there with him, a first they could share together. He squints and can see the gift shop is darker than it should be, and just then a young man pulls a gate closed across the driveway, and with a solemn shake of his head, confirms they've missed their chance today. He is caught off guard when he feels a twinge of something in his ribs. He can't help thinking that he's failed her — he knows she won't care about a place like this, but she's always asking him if there's something else they can do to get closer, to grow together — what better than himself as a child: pretending to be a conductor, train-shaped birthday cakes, his favorite gold-chrome train from his grandfather. But now they're stuck in front of the gate, looking at some tracks from the side of the road. He tried to be content, his arm curled around her, his palm resting in the space that is not quite armpit nor breast, to be content with the sensation of her breathing. She squirms, and keeps squirming, fully exasperated. He glances at her over his glasses and she starts clawing her shins, and says *mosquitoes. Aren't you getting eaten alive?* And he feels the same way he felt when his father told him he was too old for his gold train — it was a toy, for Christ's sake — and took it to an undisclosed location, most likely the trash or the Goodwill. He observes Mabel, who looks like she's playing Twister with herself, all knotted up like a contortionist. Something bad he cannot name is percolating in him, something that makes him faintly sick to be here in this place he's always wanted to see and only to have it be this. Mabel shoots straight up and points above them: a train coming into sight. He squeezes her shoulder toward him, and considers saying something clumsy about what he feels for her, which is almost always "I love you," which seems to provoke irritation in her because some Great Thinker somewhere once said something about repeated phrases losing their potency when said too often. Still, he will say it anyway, because that's what he wants to say and there is no other way to say it, even if it's rimmed with spite, but it can wait until after this train has moved out of sight and back through the leaves, into the Alleghenies. He watches the boxcars sprayed with graffiti, the mechanical components moving all that cargo across the tracks. And just like that, all that tonnage of coal or lumber or merchandise is almost gone; he can see the caboose approaching his periphery, and he is distraught at knowing this one experience is already almost over, but also considers the difference it would make — in anything, really — if he could always see the beginning and end at once.

All the Electric Novelty

i.

She has never been to Pittsburgh, so he takes her. She closes her eyes through the Squirrel Hill Tunnel, refusing to open them until she can feel the light cut through her lids and she knows for sure they're on the other side — that's the only way to earn a wish in a tunnel. She feels bad that he can't close his eyes without sending them straight into concrete, so she makes a wish on his behalf, forfeiting her own. She does not know what he would spend it on.

ii.

They ride the elevator to their hotel's third floor, and smile at the other couple in the tiny wood-paneled box. The doors recede back into the walls, and they drag their suitcases behind them to their rooms. Mabel jumps on the bed, until she suspects Andrew disapproves, but then she forgets about it, and they pull each other's clothes off like the world is ending and they don't even have time to pull back the bedspread first to do it on the sheets.

iii.

He holds her hand through the streets as she points to everything she sees with excitement. They stop in a restaurant and eat artisan pierogies, drink pint-sized cocktails until they can hardly stand. He leans over and speaks into her ear over the noise, *I never have any fun without you.* She squeezes his knee under the table. *I didn't know how to live before you.* They stagger home in the night, and collapse in their room. It feels good to be happy, if feels good to not feel unwell. They make it to the bed, onto the bedspread like before.

iv.

In the morning, they drive all over Oakland, Shadyshide, the Strip, in search of a diner that's not too crowded, that might be able to fit them in before brunch is over. They put their name in at each one, wait twenty minutes, and then cave, hoping the next location will have a shorter wait. They are hungry and a bit hungover, but she is undaunted, riding the high of all these bridges she can't tell apart, like yellow and blue ribbons lacing up the city like a present: is this Roberto Clemente, or Andy Warhol? She blurts out, *Lets go to Ohio, we're so close!*, elated at all the electric novelty. *I never want this to stop. I don't want to go back.* She is quieter, which makes it clear she is serious. She considers how far west could she go without him, what would it feel like to be the one leaving, what are the limits of this perpetual migration?

III. Bird Watching at the End of the World

A Bird in the Hand

Once—while submerged in the astonishing
blue of vinyl liner and liquid—I heard
a sound sharp enough to pierce
water, to drag me from the pool, dripping

across the scratchy grass. Beneath an oak,
a breathing clump of brownish something, maybe
a sparrow? I was ten; I did not know
names of birds or even painters—I couldn't spot

the angle of her neck and call it "Picasso-esque"
as I might now. I could hardly feel
the weight of her in my hand, her hollow bones,
matted feathers, light as a Styrofoam cup.

Letter to Descartes

"I suppose that I possess no senses; I believe that body, figure,
extension, motion, and place are merely fictions of my mind.
What is there, then, that can be esteemed true?" -Rene
Descartes

Prove to me you still never broke down
after all your calculations that only thoughts
were to be trusted, that you never asked why
God was fond of hide-and-seek. Did you
boycott candles, refuse tea, curse each beehive
for the thought of wax and its knack for versatility. Perhaps

you were mistaken all those instances you led
your daughter gently by her dainty wrist, or found
a kind of solace in watching her peek playfully
through waist-deep tulips, curving outward around
her body. She sang to herself a little something
she must have made up. It was the last memory
you had with your Francine, before her fever.

She took after you, you know: fragile health, black hair,
slender fingers. How she loved to press those hands
up to yours, to see her smaller shape a stencil
on your palm. But that's all corporeal stuff, Rene,
and it's OK if you counted over and over again

the twenty-four right angles of her tiny casket
to convince yourself that you were uncertain
if you even cried at all. Trust that I won't mention anything
if you're tempted to look back, thirsting
for sentiment, to conclude you crafted something
sacred, better than yourself, undoubtedly.

The Museum of Philosophy

Soot-stained air from extinguished candles.
A finally empty sink. An overhead light

pouring my blurred reflection into it — a halo
in the stainless steel. Sheer curtains that shine

in nylon or rayon, or some kind of manufactured
textile not found in nature, swaying from the rod;

the fleur-de-lis finials holding gathered seams
in place. A salt shaker resting on a ledge

above the stove. A salt-saliva taste that,
after much contemplation, cannot be traced

to its source. An antique desk, barren
except a vase of rubber calla lilies colored pale

celery and cream that will last forever.
At least three silverware patterns jumbled

in the kitchen drawer. A closet that must be
leaned against to close. A shelf filled with Kant,

Schopenhauer, Camus, some dog-eared paperbacks
riddled with notes written in my hand.

Was it de Beauvoir who said that the purpose
of philosophy was to soothe solitude, to prove

that others have felt the same as I do, now?
I touch the spines of hardcovers, feel

the laminated binding, and know there is no
wise passage waiting to keep me company.

Two beds, two baths; my collection of tedium
behind the glass door that I hastily unlock

each time I return—all of this, and not one
of these things capable of welcoming me home.

Aquarius

I was young enough to be unconscious
of my body, to not yet despise the look
    of my bare thick thighs doused in chlorine,
or being deemed a siren, singing
    to prove I hadn't drown. My mother,
scented coconut from tanning oil,
    closes her eyes against the summer
in a reclining plastic chair. Our skin, brown
    as paper bags, evidence of long days bathed
in searing light. I drizzle pailfuls of pool water
    to cool her flesh collecting the ultraviolet,
sneak a sip of her soda, then scurry up
    the splintered deck steps to plummet back
into the calm surface, forming my first successful dive,
    unwitnessed, in shallow water.

Eschatology

The Mylar balloons at every birthday party
will wrinkle, flatten in the exponential darkness,

suffocate air itself, fringing on our permanent
eclipse. Memory cards, computer chips, all

our little digital sequins will implode to barren ash.
The tree bark frays like banana peels, like skeletal

blossoms. I cannot fathom an end without Andrew.
The bombs, the meteorites the size of Alaska, the sun

fizzling and cooling like a spent incandescent bulb —
whatever brings us all to this unraveling, I will find

a basement where he and I can cry and watch
this world disintegrate through one tiny window

nailed shut above us, while there is still an "us"
that is tangible, two forms that can cling

through this Ultimate Tumult. His dissertation
on thermodynamics: gone. The archived footage

of every presidential speech, Aristotle's Poetics,
every love letter swept into a drainage ditch. I can't

help but feel remorse, knowing that on this day,
every idea will be vacuumed out from us and mulched

into sawdust; that this, above all, will move me.
I think of Socrates, who chose hemlock over forfeiting

the mind — how fruitless when no one is left to hear
of this. We will spend the last instant anxious

with reflection, in bitter need: reluctant, we surrender
skin to floods of violet light, hoarse prayers, paper cuts

(we always loved history, documents, all things
that made us eternal, until now). How, then,

could any of us pause for one breath, swipe soot
from each other's eyes, fumble for faint pulses

in our neighbors' necks like a lost wedding band
at the beach, when there is so little time left

to the one question we were all placed here
to uncover? One remaining typewriter on Earth,

a mechanical carcass to record our favorite postulate.
A frenzy of wry hands behave like opposing magnets.

None of us will wince, absorbed in transcription
when the ligaments of matter disband.

Einstein's Prophecy Loosely Penetrates my Nightmare

"If the bee disappeared off the surface of the globe, then man
would have only four years of life left." -Albert Einstein

In my dream, you showed me a handful
of teeth, smiled—proof they weren't yours.
You've never seen my bedroom, but here
you stood, indisputable, in that way sleep
allows everything to transform, in that way
a photo still tells the truth, even when left
in the sun for too long. The walls
were breeding wasps: they filled windows,
flickering between glass and screen, desperate.
We tore our lashes from the lids, wished
silently, focused (the way the pious
pray). You opened my window, easy
as a fortune cookie, knowing to discard
whatever hidden wisdom buzzed
inside. At my distress, you offered:
They're not bees. Useless. They'll never
yield a drop of honey.

Day Trip Alone to Shelburne, MA

These glassblowers I'm watching
treat molten sand like bubble gum — vibrant
and elastic. It's whimsical. I'm clinging
to the song of rushing water
trembling over ancient glacial spaces.
I select a bench, flip open a spiral bound

book, take notes. I'm determined, bound
to be inspired. It's almost March; I'm watching
swallows streak through clear spaces
of sky for the first time. Typically, vibrant
light doesn't first strike this pool of water
until late April, at best, winter clinging

like a bruise. Here, pollen already clings
to every surface. A mosquito pierces me, binds
her proboscis to my arm — her first flight from water
after hatching. I don't swat, allow myself to watch
as nature's first syringe draws up my vibrant
blood. Satisfied, she hovers into space.

My eyes follow her departure, think of all spaces,
wonder if maybe other beings cling
to existence elsewhere among vibrant
gases. I'm convinced there's bound
to be some lovely breed of life, watching
our blunders from afar. I approach the water

timidly, dip my hands, awestruck as water
begins filling the dimpled spaces
in my palm. I reluctantly check my watch.
Driving back, a hitch-hiker clings
to a cardboard sign: *southbound*.
His glossy eyes in headlights are vibrant

and slick as broken glass, silver coins, vibrant
as new steel guardrails. My eyes water
at my own suspicion: *he's bound*
to be dangerous. There's ample space
in the car. The rain commences. He clings
to optimism as drivers skirt past. He watches

me pleadingly, water now clinging
to his hair. In this half-vibrant world, we're bound
to each other; I hope nothing in space is watching.

Matthew

1976-1998

think breath,   contagious   as breath itself,
cascading through tissue   since birth,
since passage through fissure   of flesh,
like you.   think sweat streaking
palms   seeking solace in pockets,   a hallway
too narrow to pass.   blink fast,
clamp teeth to deny speech
or kisses   except in darkness.   think denial,
think exile,   violator   of common policy,
parody of humanity.   think stray dog,
snout in garbage,   starved,   condemned
to sustain from scraps,   forgotten
matter.   think leper,
think pus and blood   entangled
in sharp barbs of a metal fence, closely,
like lovers' legs.   think
gravel and grass,   companions
while i'm strung up in confessions
of the last sunset   while i wonder
what will they think when they write my eulogy?

The Fate of the Bee Hive Discovered in the Convent Walls

Between the feral and the house of god:
the original piñata. The hive that murmured
hymns in body language more valid and exact

than ours. Sacred, visceral. A choir singing *Einstein,*
who speculated our lost honey. They sing *warm*
and *Zen;* sing *Czar, barn,* and *learn.* Not much

sounds like *hallelujah.* They turn Spit and sugar
to sleeping bags. They must have started years ago,
back in the '50s, cubbies built thin as communion,

paper-celled hexagons. Sweet humming clump
of pipe cleaners, cellophane—a kindergarten craft—
nuzzled in drywall of a convent. How, busy as they are,

they would hum along to Sunday sermons, undetectable
against the groaning organ, the rosaries kneaded
in lassoed fingers, the morning devotional —

forgive us our trespasses, as we forgive those
who trespass against us. There is no saint
named after the mythical nymph, Melissa: Our Lady

of Perpetual Sweetness, who healed Zeus
back from the brink of death with honey.
Whole families swarmed, sought shelter

in a place whose doors remain ajar without judgment,
all silenced, each queen and drone exterminated
to cut remodeling costs $4,000.

Bird Watching at the End of the World (i)

It's not the premature heat, seething
in waves from pavement, that melts me
into anxiety. Not the conveyor belt of Vs
that flings itself north, earlier each year, its stray
feathers lost against backdrops of clouds
in alien climates. Or the sensation of not knowing
where the ocean ends: a cluster of seagulls
50 miles from any shore, loitering above
dumpsters, sneaking deep-fried remnants
clamped snugly in a beak. Not collages
of straw wrappers threading birds' nests,
built in apertures of store-front signs. No.
It's the sleek head, wings, routine undaunted,
so convinced it's always been this way.

The Statement

We came to celebrate Halloween
doused in sweat and glitter, circling
     hips in sepia light, side by side
     to strangers, feather boas
shedding and sticking to our skin.
Once exhausted, we slipped out the side door
     to drag ourselves past the dead-ends
     of the city alleys. The club music followed us
through brick walls, then merged with insults
from balconies above. I forged our damp hands
     into a knot as we trudged toward
     the car. She asked if I was nervous,
and I told her not to worry, I told her
I would protect her. But then seven of them
     leaked from the shadows and distant traffic
     racket. The first fist slammed into her jaw,
both of us thrashed to a sandpaper
sidewalk, separated by thirty feet
     of space and a ring of men: three
     to each girl, and one that floated
between us, like a spare electron, like a dog
torn between two bones. A boot was thrust
     between my breasts, shattering
     my sternum. I do not know

what prompted them to stop,
but I gathered her, limp in my arms,
    and maneuvered us to the car,
    to the hospital, propelled by shock
or strength to call you now.
                Yes, officer,
                that's all I know. No, you can't
        speak to her — the doctors are inserting
        a steel rod in her skull to hold
her jaw in place. She won't be talking
for a long time. Yes, we
      were the only witnesses.

The Girl and the Grasshopper

After plucking him from the fencepost,
she leans into small hands and almost scolds:
be thankful I stopped you from getting past

me. I'll protect you. Cupped in her hands,
like a glass ornament: neither able to withstand
the coarse touch of an eight year old

unless she's gentle. She yearns to befriend
him, watches his eyes swiveling in splinters of light
shining through the space where each finger ends.

She wonders how he'd move in flight
As she observes his legs' mechanical motion,
and then—before fascination deflates

into disgust, he spits a brown-black slime
on her skin, straight on the heartline. She sobs,
wipes her palm, chucks him to the spider's web:
this, the one defense against her first rejection.

I Must Have Been Nikola Tesla in Another Life

I want to be surrounded in yellow, like sunrise
or cheap liquid soap. Saffron; canary yellow—although
I could never need those birds like my pigeons: no one
will break their necks, eat them as aphrodisiacs
like their dove cousins. It's fine. Let me keep my pigeons.

Central Europe, Eastern Europe, where-ever—
someplace Slavic calls for me. All those former-Soviet places.
I can't explain the bruises on my calves—I suspect something
in my sleep pulls at my legs to keep me
when I'm coming back to consciousness.

I want to burrow in drywall, follow wires, uproot them
like crabgrass clogging the lawn—I know why
they're called "electrical terminals." I am tempted
to lick the wall socket, to taste the blue light. This is not
synesthesia; you are simply not understanding me.
I touch everything in grocery stores with wonder. It's never

quiet enough. I pick at my needlepoint, squinting
in dim light. I'm unable to stop talking. Let me
keep the books under my arms. I'll even surrender
all phone calls, moths humming in my ears
from the receiver. I can't tell if, in this grand river,
I'll keep alternating currents or flail until I'm pulled under.

Upon Feeding a Pigeon in New York City

I have lured her close enough to my concrete bench
to see the sheen of oily down around her throat,
the twitches of her tail skimming sidewalk grout,
her rhythmic neck a fulcrum between the hunger
inside her and the eyes searching to satisfy it. I break
a handful of crackers, leftover from lunch, and toss them.
Fascinated, I watch her waddle to my scattered crumbs,
her feet colored the flesh of a pink grapefruit. I lean
my head over to watch her, until I'm hit with the scent
of stale beer, old cola. A faint chorus of aluminum cans
chatter like cheap wind chimes. In my periphery,
a man has plunged elbow-deep into trash. Without looking—
I cannot look — I know he is unshaven and ashamed.

Circadian Rhythm

If the atmosphere dissolves, it's my fault.
I waste the meager afternoon light sprawled
out on the carpet, my shoes still on, unwashed
hair; young and unemployed and anonymous.
Each day at four, I suddenly lunge for my keys,

drive circles around the January dusk. Over
the bridge, through a neighboring state by way
of battered farmland. A flock of birds departs
from a rooftop, together but wavering like a flame,
or a blanket lifted to be spread over grass.

The elm leaves are still a muted gold; their forest
looks like bouquets of closed eyes. The pavement
erodes beneath me, potholes large enough
to lose control of the car, or concentration.
It's dark enough for streetlights, yet not for stars.

I waste gasoline and time like I can afford it. But who
knows how long this will go on for? Maybe I can.

Bird Watching at the End of the World (ii)

It starts with a certain stillness — a wing
held up at a right angle, head cocked
as if the grackle is watching me back.

It is hard to see clearly from here, but perhaps
he holds a twig in his beak, half-hanging
like a cigarette. Today is overcast but shows

no sign of rain; the grackle's slick black feathers
turn matte under the burlap sky. I have always
imagined that it would be different, that I could expect

sirens and flames, a pathological need to call
everyone I know and tell them for the last time
why I love them: my mother for her chronic nostalgia,

my father for his indignation at kitsch, my lover
who feared no consequence was so grave
as that of being idle. But it is not so. I watch

this grackle, the sagging boughs of white pine
he rests on, and know this from the way nothing
possesses urgency at all, that not one feather

or small eye reflects any light, no pane of glass
from the neighborhood's windows mirror
the world back in outlines of glare, as ghosts.

It is upon us. I was expecting a short fuse
and a loud bang. Of course it is this very lack
of vigor in all things that informs me of this ending.

It is this slow wilt, this calm unlacing of the corset
that holds the world together — that we have always
been slouching towards entropy, without noticing.

The Bridge at Winchester

"I do not conceive of any reality at all as without genuine
unity." -Gottfried Leibniz

I can see at the bottom
of the clouded stream of ochre
two ancient bicycles, chainless
and abandoned, countless clots
of rotting leaves, a shovel

someone will miss in the coming
months of New Hampshire winter.
Water glides over the debris.
A lone goose, divided from his letter
formation, laments over and over—

perhaps because he is lost, perhaps
as a retaliation against their leaving.
The sky sounds like a one-note solo
of a badly-bent trombone.
I admire the ubiquitous indifference

of nature: such fortitude, such
restraint it must take, to be the medium
for all these misplaced things. I spit
my gum, long devoid of flavor, off
the side of this nameless pedestrian

bridge into the river. When the water calms,
I spot the reflection of two maple branches,
Thin as popsicle sticks, arc across the water
from opposite riverbanks, as if extending
to connect and can't quite reach.

Boundary

=

On the other side of the river,
train tracks form a flattened
ladder: wooden railroad ties
perpendicular to the twin
steel rails, parallel for miles
and never allowed to touch each other.

= =

At the adjacent gas station,
a drowsy stubbled man slouches
behind the white counter, on which
a bucket of cellophane wrapped
roses made of felt paper is displayed.

A woman speaks to him
through a plexiglas window
and pays for coffee. It is unclear
if it is breath or steam rising

from the paper cup that forms
a foggy nebula of condensation
between them, their eyes focused

on the coins they exchanged
without grazing the other's hand.

= = =

How far away is air before it is considered sky?

Lisa Mangini holds an MFA from Southern Connecticut State University. She is the author of three chapbooks: *Slouching Towards Entropy* (Finishing Line Press), *Perfect Objects in Motion* (Red Bird Chapbooks), and *Immanuel Kant vs. God* (Red Bird Chapbooks). She teaches English composition and creative writing part-time at Southern Connecticut State University and Asnuntuck Community College; she is also the Founding Editor of *Paper Nautilus*. She was raised in Enfield, Connecticut, where she lives still, traveling frequently to Central Pennsylvania. This is her first full-length collection.

CPSIA information can be obtained at www.ICGtesting.com
Printed in the USA
BVOW03s0947201114

375866BV00007B/125/P